LEARNING OBJECTIVES FOR:

POWERFUL PROOFREADING SKILLS

The objectives for *Powerful Proofreading Skills* are listed below. They have been developed to guide you, the reader, to the core issues covered in this book.

Objectives

❑ 1) **To present helpful hints for successful proofreading**

❑ 2) **To provide training in correct grammar, punctuation, spelling, usage, capitalization, and numbers**

❑ 3) **To give proofreading practice**

Assessing Your Progress

In addition to the learning objectives, Crisp, Inc. has developed an **assessment** that covers the fundamental information presented in this book. A twenty-five item, multiple choice/true-false question-naire allows the reader to evaluate his or her comprehension of the subject matter. An answer sheet with a chart matching the questions to the listed objectives is also available. To learn how to obtain a copy of this assessment please call: **1-800-442-7477** and ask to speak with a Customer Service Representative.

Assessments should not be used in any selection process.

PREFACE

Proofreading! Ugh, you're thinking! Are you saying right now, "I don't like to proofread," "It's boring," "I don't have time," or "So what if an error appears in a document as long as my reader understands what I say"? All right! We know that proofreading is not the most exciting subject in the world, but it is an essential skill in writing. And the better writer you are, the more valuable you are to your manager and your organization.

Unlike many subjects, proofreading is not a theoretical topic. It's concrete— specific—comprised of "how to's." The rules and guidelines we'll offer you are simple and practical. You'll have a chance to check your understanding and evaluate your progress in each section of this book. Practice is the key; we'll give you plenty of exercises along the way.

We believe that people learn faster and retain information longer when they are having fun. That's what we want for you. So our goal in the pages that follow is to make the proofreading tips, techniques, and tactics enjoyable and memorable and to make you a stronger and more effective proofreader. We hope you share this goal with us.

Here's to becoming a powerful proofreader. Enjoy!

Debra A. Smith   Helen R. Sutton

POWERFUL PROOFREADING SKILLS
Tips, Techniques and Tactics

Debra A. Smith
Helen R. Sutton

A FIFTY-MINUTE™ SERIES BOOK

CRISP PUBLICATI~~ONS~~
Menlo Park, Califor~~nia~~

POWERFUL PROOFREADING SKILLS

Tips, Techniques and Tactics

Debra A. Smith
Helen R. Sutton

CREDITS
Managing Editor: **Kathleen Barcos**
Editor: **Elaine Brett**
Typesetting: **ExecuStaff**
Cover Design: **Fifth Street Design**
Artwork: **Ralph Mapson**

© 1994 by Crisp Publications, Inc.
Printed in the United States of America by Bawden Printing Company.

http://www.crisp-pub.com

Distribution to the U.S. Trade:

National Book Network, Inc.
4720 Boston Way
Lanham, MD 20706
1-800-462-6420

98 99 00 01   10 9 8 7 6 5 4 3 2

Library of Congress Catalog Card Number 93-73201
Smith, Debra A. and Helen R. Sutton
Powerful Proofreading Skills
ISBN 1-56052-259-3

This book is printed on recyclable paper with soy ink.

PRINTED WITH
SOY INK

ABOUT THE AUTHORS

Debra A Smith is a nationally respected consultant, speaker, and seminar leader. Every year she travels to over 100 cities in the United States and Canada to deliver her seminars on communication, time management, conflict resolution, stress management, and customer relations.

She has served as business manager for a management consulting group where she was responsible for financial accountability and customer relations. She holds a B.A. in management and an M.B.A. degree in management from Golden Gate University.

Debra is the author of the CareerTrack Seminars, Inc. audio and videotape programs on *Professional Telephone Skills, Powerful Presentation Skills*, and *Business Writing Skills*. She also is the co-author of their *Proofreading and Editing Skills* videotape program.

Helen R. Sutton has taught business English, writing, and reading for more than a decade. She has served as a training manager for a national seminar company where she developed and coordinated in-house training for a staff of over 400. She also has designed and implemented curricula for public and private seminars.

She has been a program development specialist/training manager with Career Track Seminars, Inc. where she produced their videotape programs, *Proofreading and Editing Skills* and *How to Be a Better Trainer*. She has written articles for *Careers and the M.B.A.* magazine.

Helen is an internationally acclaimed consultant and seminar leader. She speaks on the topics of self-esteem, communication, and writing and editing in the United States, Canada, the United Kingdom, and Asia.

CONTENTS

Introduction ix

Proofreader's Pretest x

SECTION I   PROOFREADING FOR ERROR-FREE COPY 1
What Is Proofreading? 3
Setting the Stage 6
Getting Started 7
Achieving Error-free Documents 9
Proofreading Numbers and Names 14
Incorporating Proofreaders' Marks 18
How to Give Proofreading Feedback to Others 22

SECTION II   PROOFREADING FOR ACCURACY 25
Know Your Grammar Terms 27
Proofreading for Grammatical Errors 29
Proofreading for Punctuation Errors 43
Proofreading for Spelling Errors 54
Proofreading for Usage Errors 58
Proofreading for Capitalization Errors 63
Proofreading for Number Errors 70

SECTION III   SUMMARY 73
Proofreader's Post Test 75
Create Your Own Proofreader's Library 76

SECTION IV   EXERCISE ANSWERS 77
Recommended Reading 94

Powerful Proofreading Skills

INTRODUCTION

Welcome to *Powerful Proofreading Skills.* The days of embarrassing, mistake-ridden documents are about to come to an end! How? By reading the pages and working the exercises you'll find in this action-packed training resource. This proofreading reference is designed to give you the knowledge and skills necessary to produce error-free copy in written correspondence and documents.

Accuracy in today's office documents—memos, letters, reports, and proposals—is critical because it reflects an organization's commitment to quality. You'll be able to achieve this accuracy if you commit to learning and then using the guidelines and stategies offered to you. In each section you'll find exercises and activities that will strengthen your proofreading ability in such troublesome areas as grammar, punctuation, spelling and usage, capitalization, and numbers. You'll learn the rules that are appropriate and correct for today's office communication and how to avoid the blunders that cost time and money.

Powerful Proofreading Skills is not only useful for individual study, but it is also ideal as a resource guide in workshops and seminars and as a desk reference. However you choose to use it, this book will help you polish your proofreading skills and enhance your ability to express yourself like a pro.

So, let's get started.

PROOFREADER'S PRETEST

OK proofreaders, let's get started! What better place to begin than with a pretest. Take a few minutes to answer the following ten questions, which are representative of the areas that we'll cover in *Powerful Proofreading Skills*. When you're finished, you'll find the answers on pages 79–80. Good luck!

1. _____ is the correct proofreaders' mark to indicate "delete copy."

    a. ≡   b. ℘   c. ∪̂   d. ∿

2. _____ is the correct proofreaders' mark to indicate "capitalize."

    a. ≡   b. ℘   c. ∪̂   d. ∿

3. Underline the letters that should be capitalized in the following sentences:

    the repair person flew in from the west coast to repair our xerox copier.

    susan james, director of the new york theatre company, addressed the cast of the phantom of the opera.

4. Correctly punctuate the following sentences:

    Mr Lewis was late to the meeting he was on a conference call with an important client

    Ms Solomonson said Grace I want you to meet with the doctors from San Francisco Austin Denver Chicago and Boston on September 22 1995

5. Please circle all misspelled words in the following sentences:

    We recieved the goverment questionaire and immediately returned it.

    The unanamous decision was delivered at the begining of the meeting by the marketing commitee.

    Our third quarter calender will accomodate your scheduleing needs immediatly.

6. Please circle the correct word from each pair in the following sentences:

There seems to be a conflict (among, between) sales and marketing.

The (perspective, prospective) clients will fly in tomorrow to meet with our customer service representatives.

The computer training will (precede, proceed) the actual installation of the Macintosh equipment.

7. *True or False:* It is very difficult to use a partner when you are proofreading; it is best to proofread on your own.

8. *True or False:* One proofreading strategy—distance *yourself*—means to hold your hard copy an arm's length away from you while you proofread it.

9. Which sentence is correct? Underline either *a* or *b*.

a. The company will distribute its annual report tomorrow.
b. The company will distribute their annual report tomorrow.

a. Either the computer or the typewriter are to be moved to the adjoining office.
b. Either the computer or the typewriter is to be moved to the adjoining office.

a. The box containing all the office supplies is stored in the spare room.
b. The box containing all the office supplies are stored in the spare room.

10. Please list five ways to overcome the tedium (pain!) of proofreading long documents.

a.

b.

c.

d.

e.

SECTION

I

Proofreading for Error-Free Copy

WHAT IS PROOFREADING?

In a nutshell, proofreading is producing error-free copy or achieving 100 percent accuracy in your correspondence. As a proofreader, you have one objective in mind—to make sure the copy you have created matches the original document in its intended form or to make sure the document you have composed is accurate. Now what do we mean by accurate? Ask yourself if you verified accuracy in all of these areas:

- ► Sentence structure
- ► Grammar
- ► Punctuation
- ► Spelling and usage
- ► Capitalization
- ► Numbers

How Does Proofreading Differ from Editing?

Good question! Good editors are good proofreaders, but they have additional responsibilities. Editors also evaluate the style and format of a document and make the necessary changes. When you edit, your objective is to make sure the document reflects these six characteristics:

- • Clear

- • Concise

- • Coherent

- • Concrete

- • Considerate

- • Complete

You will engage in actual rewriting when you are editing—but not when you are proofreading.

WHAT IS PROOFREADING? (continued)

Let's make sure this is clear. Here's an example—using the same sentence—of how proofreading differs from editing.

- **Original Sentence:**

  I would like to take this oportunity to think you for agreeing to meet with me on Tuesday, October 29th.

- **Proofreading Correction:**

  I would like to take this opportunity *to* thank *you for agreeing to meet with me on Tuesday, October* 29.

- **Editing Correction:**

  Thank you for agreeing to meet with me on Tuesday, October 29.

Notice the difference. In the proofreading correction, the text remains the same, but we fixed the spelling and number errors. In the editing correction, we noticed that the sentence was too wordy; "I would like to take this opportunity" is unnecessary. The sentence is strengthened when we begin with "Thank you."

What Are the Benefits of Learning This Valuable Skill?

There are a lot of benefits! If you're known in your organization as a top-notch proofreader, you become much more visible. People will see you as a communication expert and that can lead to promotional opportunities. Your credibility will be strengthened, and your professional image will be enhanced. The more proofreading you do, the more you will learn about your position, your department, and your organization. And remember, knowledge is power! You'll find that more and more people will come to you with their questions about how to write or say something. They will accept your answers and trust you to know what is right. You will attain "expert" power, and if you use it wisely, you can give your career a big boost.

Benefits of Learning Proofreading Skills

✔ **Credibility**

✔ **Image**

✔ **Organizational Knowledge**

✔ **Work Variety**

✔ **Career Opportunities**

✔ **Expert Power**

SETTING THE STAGE

*"A good business letter can get you a job interview,
get you off the hook, or get you money. It's totally asinine to
blow your chances of getting whatever you want with a
business letter that turns people off instead of turning them on."*

—Malcolm Forbes

Check all that apply:

☐ Have you ever typed a document, proofed it, printed it, and then caught an error?

☐ Have you corrected that error, printed the document again, and then caught another error?

☐ Have you ever proofed a document more than once and still missed an error?

☐ Have you ever read through a document, not finding any errors, then asked a colleague to read it, and he or she immediately spotted an error?

☐ Have you ever printed multiple copies, distributed them, and then found an error?

If you answered "yes" to any of these (and we bet you have), help is on the way! Review the upcoming proofreading tips and strategies thoroughly. What changes do you need to make to improve the accuracy of your proofreading?

GETTING STARTED

► Determine when you are "at your best" or most alert. You'll do a better job proofreading and catching errors.

► Remove as many distractions as you can. If possible, close your door, forward your calls, and clear other projects from your desk area. The more you can concentrate on *just proofreading*, the more success you'll have.

► Keep all important reference materials within arm's reach. Don't keep getting up and down to gather resources. A dictionary and a business reference guide are a must!

► Before you begin, know all timelines, due dates, and deadlines. This will help you plan and budget your time well and prevent the rush of proofreading a document at the last minute.

► For longer documents or for multiple bosses, use a style sheet showing word style decisions you make and preferences each one has.

► Show your co-workers the proofreading marks you will be using. Make sure everyone is using the same system.

► As best as you can, sit in a comfortable chair of the correct height, use adequate lighting that's easy on your eyes, and maintain good posture.

GETTING STARTED (continued)

Beating Those Proofreading Blues

- Take short breaks when you proofread for long periods of time.

- Exercise regularly—stretch your neck, arms, and shoulders.

- Eat light meals as needed. Avoid heavy foods that are sure to make you tired.

- Ask a partner to assist you when you proofread lengthy, highly technical, or complicated material.

- Rest your eyes for 30 seconds every 10 to 15 minutes.

- When you become tired or bored, change activities.

Proofreading "Musts"

✓ Accuracy is your top priority—speed must come second (even when you're in a hurry!).

✓ Plan to proofread each document at least three times. It may sound like a lot, but you'll catch all the errors and avoid costly corrections.

✓ When you proofread numbers, read aloud—digit by digit.

✓ Place a straightedge (ruler, piece of paper) below the line you are reading to avoid skipping words or lines of text.

✓ Distance yourself from any document *you* just composed. It is common to miss mistakes in work you produced. Whenever possible, put time between the writing and the proofreading stages. When you return to correct your work, you'll be more objective.

✓ Double-space documents in draft form for easy proofreading.

ACHIEVING ERROR-FREE DOCUMENTS

Comparison Method

Position the original document close to the updated or corrected copy. Move your eyes back and forth between the two. Hold your fingers or a pen/pencil on the original and corrected copy and follow along as you read. Remember—proofreading is not a spectator sport; it takes effort and action on your part! If you are proofing an original document and your corrected copy is still on your computer screen, hold your original next to the screen. Again, keep your finger or a pen on the hard copy and run your cursor down the computer screen. Sometimes it's possible to set the original on top of the corrected copy and hold both up to the light. Any discrepancies can be seen by using this technique.

Be careful not to lose your place. Avoid distractions as much as possible. Errors occur when you take your eyes and your attention off your copy.

Proofing with a Partner—The Comparative Method

One partner checks the final copy while the other is reading aloud. The partner method is best when important material must be proofed. This is a convenient way to double-check your work as you proofread. Long columns of numbers are often best proofed with a partner.

One drawback—partner proofing takes the time of two people away from their other tasks. Make sure you select a partner who is also a good proofreader!

Reading Aloud

When you read aloud or move your lips and form each word, you are forced to slow down and read each word. You *hear* and listen for sentence correctness.

ACHIEVING ERROR-FREE DOCUMENTS
(continued)

Visual Proofreading

To check the alignment of your document, use these three techniques:

- Hold the document at arm's length.

- Turn it upside down.

- Lay a straightedge on the left and right margins.

Read the Document Backward

Reading material from right to left or from the bottom of the page to the top forces you to look at individual words. Reading backward helps when you are checking details such as spelling; however, it is not effective for checking content accuracy.

IDENTIFYING ERROR "HOT SPOTS"

Proofreading errors are found often:

► Near the beginning or ending of a line

► In proper nouns

► In long words

► Near the bottom of the page

► In number combinations

► In titles and headings

► In names

Watch for the following errors:

► Doubling small words (if, in, as, by, be)

► Omission of one of a pair of doubled letters (omitted)

► Substitution of one small word for another (an for on, in for on, by for be)

► Transposition of words within sentences

► Transposition of letters within words

► Omission of a closing quotation mark, bracket, or parenthesis

► Words such as *if, in, is,* and *it* left out when the preceding word ends with the same letter or the next word begins with it

► Confusion of suffixes (for example, typed/types, former/formed)

► Missing numbers or letters in a sequence: G, H, J, K, or 15, 17, 18

PROOFREADING FROM A COMPUTER SCREEN

► When proofreading on-screen, slowly scroll your document down line by line on the first reading. Or use a straightedge against the screen to prevent your eyes from darting.

► When proofreading hard copy produced on a word processor, keep your screen and hard copy at the same place in the document. Corrections and updates will be easier and faster.

► Hold the original next to the computer screen and use the comparison method of proofreading.

► When proofreading on-screen, enlarge the type you are reading. Errors are more likely to stand out in a larger type font.

► Be sure to use a spell-checker and grammar checker to verify the accuracy of your writing. However, neither of these programs can take the place of proofreading.

► To increase accuracy, print a double-spaced copy of the on-screen text, and proofread from the printout. It's easier on your eyes, and you will be less distracted.

Proofreading Pointers

✓ If you are proofreading a form letter, carefully read the first letter printed out. Then proofread just the changes in all future letters.

✓ When you proofread copy transcribed from dictation equipment, return to the start of the tape and read the document as you listen to the tape.

Proofreading Strategies Assessment Scale

As you review the proofreading guidelines, evaluate how often you practice the ideas. Answer the following questions according to how often the behavior actually occurs.

Do You . . .	Always	Occasionally	Never
1. Proofread when you are most alert?	☐	☐	☐
2. Reduce distractions when you are proofreading?	☐	☐	☐
3. Have a dictionary and reference guide within arm's reach?	☐	☐	☐
4. Verify timelines, due dates, and deadlines with the person assigning the project?	☐	☐	☐
5. Arrange your proofreading setting to be physically comfortable?	☐	☐	☐
6. Take needed breaks when you feel tired?	☐	☐	☐
7. Use a partner when you proofread technical or complicated material?	☐	☐	☐
8. Proofread a document more than once?	☐	☐	☐
9. Slow down your reading rate when proofreading?	☐	☐	☐
10. Use a straightedge when proofing columns?	☐	☐	☐

PROOFREADING NUMBERS AND NAMES

The most common error you'll find when you proofread is a number or word that is simply typed wrong. This is commonly called a "typo" (typographical error), and it is usually a one-letter or one-digit mistake. You may transpose a number or a letter, omit or add a character, or simply make a misstroke. To eliminate typos from your correspondence, follow these suggestions.

Numbers

- Never assume that a number is typed correctly.

- Read once through your document just to verify numbers.

- Check each number, and make sure it's logical. (The fourth quarter, 1959 sales results will be ready next week. It should, of course, read *1995*.)

- When you proof columns of numbers, add the numbers in the original and then the final copy. Your totals should be the same.

- Make sure decimals are aligned in columns of numbers.

Names

- Read through your document once just to verify names. (People hate to see their names spelled incorrectly!)

- Check for possible alternate spellings of names (Steven or Stephen, Terri or Terry).

- Use appropriate courtesy titles (Ms., Miss, Mrs., Mr., Dr.).

- Check the spelling of each part of a person's name (first, middle, last).

Telephone Numbers

- Break the number into its parts (area code, first three digits, final four digits, extension).

- Read aloud with a partner to check phone numbers.

- Anticipate and check for transpositions.

- Line up columns of phone numbers and check the parentheses, hyphens, spaces, and digits.

OOPS! WATCH THE TYPOS

Imagine these real-life bloopers (we mean typos) appearing in newspapers, letters, ads, and signs. If you were the author, what would your readers' reaction be to you and your organization?

From a newspaper:

We very much regret our error in yesterday's edition in which we most unfortunately referred to the defective branch of the police force. We meant, of course, the detective branch of the police farce.

From a letter to a governor:

We would very much appreciate being present with the authors on the occasion of the singing of their bill.

From an excuse note received by a teacher:

Please excuse Lauree Olsen from school. She has very loose vowels.

From a classified ad:

Great Dames for sale.

From a pharmacy:

Look for prescription drugs on which the patients have expired.

From an oil and gas company:

Scientists can develop computer programs that stimulate oil reserves.

From a memo printed on letterhead:

The Great Steal of the State of Utah.

So how do you avoid these amusing, but bruising, errors?
Consider this recommendation:

The best way to find an error is to print 3,000 copies!

(A lot of help we are!)

✍ EXERCISE ONE—CHARACTER ACCURACY

Are both columns the same? Using the left column as your master, correct the differences in the right column. See pages 81–82 for answers.

PART A—Names and Telephone Numbers

Ms. Hazel Manning-Smith	Ms. Hazel Manning-Smith
(303) 321-1667	(303) 312-1667
Dr. Kim Chong	Dr. Kim Chang
(402) 346-1926	(402 346-1926
Mr. Russell Graham	Mr. Russ. L. Graham
(208) 722-4547	(208) 772-4745
Mrs. F. A. Lewis	Ms. F. A. Lewis
(203) 922-8454	(203) 922-8454
Mr. Albert Sanchez	Albert Sanchez
(616) 232-1917	(661) 232-1719
Miss Grace Bornheim	Ms. Grace Bornhiem
(316) 477-2332	(316) 447-2332
Mr. Washington Jones	Mr. Washington Jones
(701) 932-1112	(701) 932-1112
Ms. C. Anne Solomonson	Ms. Anne C. Solomonson
(503) 576-8931	(305) 576-8931
Miss Ann L. Schatz	Ms. Ann L. Schatz
(704) 883-3227	(704) 838-3227
Dr. Marin Alsop	Marin A. Alsop
(402) 728-7866	(402) 728-7866

PART B—*Invoice Numbers, Measurements, and Account Numbers*

January 1 and June 28	January 11 and June 28
ACCT. NO. HRS38930T	ACCT. NO. HRS38930T
Invoice # 125-89-RZD	Invoice # 125-98-RZD
24% increase 16% decrease	42% increase 16% decrease
February 27, 1959, at 4:32 a.m.	February 27, 1958, at 4:32 a.m.
5" x 19" and 23' x 44'	5" x 23" and 19' x 44'
ACCT. NO. (150M) 7224547 P	ACCT. NO. (150N) 7224547 P
493257.665	493257.665
13 1/3 boxes/item #78L	13 1/3 boxes/item #L78
31st of December	31st of December

INCORPORATING PROOFREADERS' MARKS

Think of proofreaders' marks as shorthand symbols that are universally recognized. These marks substitute for many words and quickly and clearly identify the corrections that need to be made in copy. They serve as an important communication link between you and anyone else reviewing the copy. It's important that everyone in your office uses the same marks to avoid confusion. To make sure everyone is speaking the same language, make a copy of the list on the next page and distribute it to your proofreading partners.

Ode to the Typographical Error

Paris

in the

the Spring

The typographical error is a slippery thing and sly;

You can hunt 'til you are dizzy, but it somehow will get by.

'Til the forms are on the press, it is strange how still it keeps.

It shrinks down in a corner, and it never stirs or peeps.

That typographical error, too small for human eyes—

'Til the ink is on the paper, then it grows to mountain size.

The boss, she stares with horror, then she grabs her hair and groans;

The copyreader drops his head upon his hands and moans.

The remainder of the issue may be clean as clean can be,

But the typographical error is the only thing you see.

—Anonymous

Can you spot the one typographical error?

Proofreaders' Marks

Mark	Meaning	Example
ℒ	Delete the word or line	Delete the word ~~computer.~~
/	Strike through the misstroke; write the correct letter above	Observe good rol̸ models. (e)
#	Insert a space	The words ran̸together.
◡	Close up the space	Mar keting goals were m et.
∽	Transpose the word or letter	Was date the postponed?
⊙ ⌃ ⌄	Insert punctuation	She left for the meeting⊙
⌃	Insert a word(s)	Her training ⌃excellent. (was)
≡	Capitalize	cindy discussed her goals with debra and helen.
lc	Put in lowercase letters	Submit your application for the lc Spring conference.
¶	Start a new paragraph	¶ We provide these services.
NO ¶	Remove the paragraph indent	NO ¶ The information was accurate.
◯	Spell out	The ③ new members were present.
SS[	Single-space	SS[Plan to order additional equipment for the office.
DS[	Double-space	DS[We will hire two new staff members for accounting.
‖	Align vertically	‖ TO: Patricia A. Ward FROM: Dr. S. Kramer
...	Stet (leave copy as it was originally)	~~Sales~~ results were late. ...

✍ EXERCISE TWO—USING PROOFREADERS' MARKS

Using the following proofreaders' marks, make the necessary corrections in the text. See page 83 for answers.

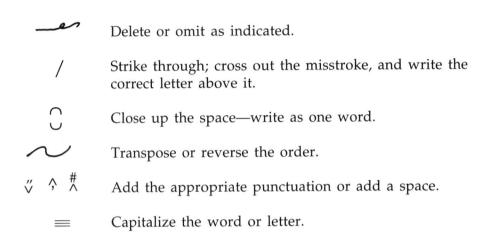

~~	Delete or omit as indicated.
/	Strike through; cross out the misstroke, and write the correct letter above it.
⌒	Close up the space—write as one word.
~	Transpose or reverse the order.
⌄ ⌃ ⌗	Add the appropriate punctuation or add a space.
≡	Capitalize the word or letter.

The most common error that you—the proofreader—will find is a typographical error. A "typo" occurs when exttra letters, spac es, figures, or copy is is added or omitted from document. Another typo results from transposign (reversing) lettres or words. (Will you practice your delete stroke now and delete this entire line of text. Thank you.)

Yuo remember must to slow down your read ing rate to spot typographical errors. It is tenmpting to rush through your documents to to save time; however, in the llong run, you'll save timew and ensure accuracy if you read carefully

in addition, it is helpful to use a standard set of proofreaders' marks when you are correcting copy. They are ti me-savers, and they keep your copy "clean." you'll be able to go back and see your original maerterial as well as your corrections!

Look out for those typos and have fnu producing etrror-free copy!

✍ EXERCISE THREE—PROOFREADERS' MARKS REVIEW

Match the mark to its meaning by placing the letter of the correct mark on the line next to each term. See page 84 for answers.

_____	**1.** STET	A. ∿
_____	**2.** Start a new paragraph	B. ≡
_____	**3.** Close up the space	C. ⋯
_____	**4.** Delete	D. *lc*
_____	**5.** Capitalize	E. DS[
_____	**6.** Spell out	F. ℯ
_____	**7.** Insert punctuation	G. ⌒⌣
_____	**8.** Transpose	H. ⊙ ⌃ ⌄
_____	**9.** Double-space	I. ¶
_____	**10.** Lowercase	J. ⬭

Quick Tips

✓ Place your proofreading marks so that they do not cover the original text.

✓ Use a contrasting color of ink to make corrections.

HOW TO GIVE PROOFREADING FEEDBACK TO OTHERS

Uh, oh! You've found a mistake or perhaps several mistakes in the copy you've been proofreading. Correcting the errors is a step in the right direction. But it's also appropriate to give feedback to the writer. How do you do this? Remember to use courtesy and diplomacy, and follow these five steps.

1. Let people save face.

Instead of: There are four typos in this letter. Can't you do anything right?

Say: There are four typos in this letter. Let's see if we can fix them. I appreciate your correcting them.

2. Focus on specific, observable behavior—not judgment or personality.

Instead of: This letter is a mess.

Say: The heading needs to be centered, and the right margin needs to be justified.

3. Don't generalize.

Instead of: You never proofread any of your work.

Say: It looks as if you did not finish proofreading the last page of the weekly status report.

4. Tell people if errors exist.

If you don't tell them, how can they improve?

5. Avoid nitpicking or overusing your power.

The objective is to produce error-free copy—not to humiliate or discount people and their work.

Giving Feedback to Your Boss

And what if it's your boss to whom you need to give feedback about errors? Keep these suggestions in mind.

► Clarify your authority. Are you to edit or proofread the copy?

► Keep a style sheet on each person who gives you correspondence to review. Write down each person's preferences.

► Avoid trapping or embarrassing the person.

Word Search Game

Proofreading can feel like looking for a needle in a haystack; you're looking for a "small" error in lines and lines of text.

Word search puzzles are solved using a similar principle. You're looking for a specific word hidden among random letters. Perhaps the better skilled you are at word search puzzles, the easier your proofreading will become!

Have some fun with this learning tool. Circle each word as you find it. Remember that 100 percent accuracy is our goal!

```
A  G  E  E  F  B  C  E  D  F  T  K  H  L
D  C  A  P  I  T  A  Z  P  N  Y  R  C  A
F  G  C  J  G  S  S  L  E  K  P  A  M  V
P  R  T  U  U  K  V  R  Q  Z  G  M  T  G
Z  A  T  I  R  Q  G  X  H  R  W  N  Z  I
S  M  B  Z  E  A  W  G  E  C  U  O  H  L
P  M  F  H  S  X  C  E  P  E  B  I  L  E
E  A  L  T  Z  F  M  Y  W  F  G  T  S  P
L  R  H  C  D  E  F  M  Z  J  Z  A  D  S
L  P  R  O  N  O  U  N  S  O  Q  U  S  N
I  P  V  T  L  N  W  O  P  K  P  T  H  U
N  W  U  Y  S  Z  P  Y  D  I  X  C  C  O
G  Q  K  O  C  J  T  S  K  V  J  N  T  P
E  F  D  B  P  X  T  L  H  B  Z  U  A  R
N  O  I  T  A  Z  I  L  A  T  I  P  A  C
```

1. PUNCTUATION MARK   6. PRONOUNS

2. CAPITALIZATION   7. FIGURES

3. AGREEMENT   8. USAGE

4. ACCURACY   9. GRAMMAR

5. TYPO   10. SPELLING

S E C T I O N

II

Proofreading for Accuracy

KNOW YOUR GRAMMAR TERMS

It's important to proofread documents for grammatical accuracy. You may be thinking, "Oh no, not grammar. I hated grammar in school. I can't remember anything!" Don't worry—it's been a few years since most of us have had a grammar class. Let's take a stroll down memory lane together. Review the terms commonly associated with grammar. We've included a definition and examples for each.

Adjective: A modifier that describes nouns

    EXAMPLES: *three* pages, *blue* folder, *competent* manager

Adverb: A modifier that describes verbs, adjectives, and other adverbs

    EXAMPLES: typed *quickly*, change occurred *slowly*, she speaks *well*

Antecedent: A noun to which a pronoun refers

    EXAMPLE: *Mary* paid her fee on Monday.

Clause: A group of related words that contains a subject and a verb. An independent clause expresses a complete thought and can stand alone as a sentence. A dependent clause does not express a complete thought and cannot stand alone as a sentence.

    EXAMPLES: (independent clause) We are not able to provide a quote for this group; (dependent clause) If you complete this form

Conjunction: A connecting word

    EXAMPLES: and, or, but, neither, nor

Interjection: Expresses exclamation

    EXAMPLES: Wow! Help! Fire!

Modifier: A word, clause, or phrase that describes a word Adjectives and adverbs are examples of modifiers.

    EXAMPLES: The *handsome, wealthy* man walked *quickly* into the *cold, dimly lit* boardroom.

Noun: Person, place, thing, object, idea

    EXAMPLES: computer, secretary, Ms. Jackson, office

KNOW YOUR GRAMMAR TERMS (continued)

Object: Follows and receives the action of the verb
To determine the object, after the verb ask "what" or "whom."

EXAMPLE: We purchased a *microcomputer*.

Phrase: A group of related words that does not contain a subject and a verb or that does not express a complete thought

EXAMPLE: Listening to what is being said

Preposition: A function word that shows relationship

EXAMPLES: to, at, by, for, on

Pronoun: Takes the place of a noun

EXAMPLES: I, she, him, we, them

Sentence: A group of words that includes a subject and a verb and states a complete thought

EXAMPLE: In today's business world, the success of your organization depends on how well you treat your customers.

Subject: The person, thing, or idea the sentence is about; a fundamental element in a sentence

EXAMPLE: The financial *analyst* examined the report.

Verb: Expresses action, condition, or state of being

EXAMPLES: writes, am, is, documents, transcribes

PROOFREADING FOR GRAMMATICAL ERRORS

"How well we communicate is determined not by how well we say things but by how well we are understood."

—Andrew S. Grove, CEO, Intel Corporation

In both speaking and writing, you express your thoughts, feelings, and beliefs in the form of sentences. To review, a *sentence* is a group of words that has a subject and a verb and expresses a complete thought. The *subject* is the person, thing, or idea being described, and the *verb* shows what the subject is or does. For short, readable sentences, keep the average sentence length at 15 to 17 words or fewer.

When you are thinking of several things at the same time and different thoughts go through your mind, it is easy to make mistakes—in fact, whole sentences can go awry. Two construction problems that frequently occur in writing are the sentence fragment and the run-on sentence.

Sentence Fragments

An incomplete sentence, called a sentence fragment, may contain both a subject and a verb but does not express a complete thought.

Fragment: When the manager called me this morning.

Sentence: When the manager called me this morning, I was surprised.

Run-On Sentences

Two or more complete ideas (sentences) that are run together with no punctuation or spacing to separate them are called a run-on sentence.

Run-on: We have only three days until the annual meeting I don't have the annual report completed and that will take at least two days to finalize.

Sentence: We have only three days until the annual meeting, and I don't have the annual report completed. It will take at least two days to finalize the report.

✍ EXERCISE FOUR—SENTENCE STRUCTURE

Read the following letter. Underline any run-on sentences, and double-underline any sentence fragments. See page 85 for answers.

Dear Mr. Grass:

I received your estimate of $1,500 for the landscaping of our property and find it to be acceptable except for the charges for rearranging the flower beds and relocating the sprinkler system we want it to cover the lawn and the flower beds and the surrounding shrubs that border our property and that of our neighbor. We will expect to see you. On July 10 at our house on Jacobson Drive so we can discuss the work in more detail. Please bring your sketches of the layout because we want to see the details of the landscaping including the colors of the flowers and the types of shrubs you plan to plant after we have approved the layout you can then proceed to complete the landscaping. Please give me a call within the next few days because we need to review the flower beds and sprinkler system so that you can explain the estimates relating to these two items they seem to be somewhat excessive considering the size of our property which is not that large. Call me before 3 p.m. On Tuesday and Wednesday I will be available. Looking forward to meeting with you.

Sincerely,

Sam Spruce

SUBJECT/VERB AGREEMENT

The most common grammatical error made in today's business correspondence is the misuse of subjects and verbs. Subjects and verbs must be
positioned in each sentence in such a way as to convey clear and accurate
meaning. Have you ever heard someone say, "I seen him down the hall"?
The problem here is subject and verb agreement (actually disagreement!).
Certainly this sounds awkward or incorrect. Imagine seeing it in a business
document! Your credibility would be blown! So proofreaders beware, and
study these agreement guidelines.

Guidelines for Subject/Verb Agreement

▶ **The subject and verb must agree in number.**
   **A singular subject must have a singular verb, and a plural subject must
   have a plural verb.**

   A price list (*subject*) is (*verb*) enclosed.
   The firms (*subject*) are (*verb*) the best in the field.

▶ **The subject and the verb must agree in number even though they may
   be separated by intervening phrases and clauses.**

   The briefcase containing the missing reports is being delivered this afternoon.
   Money, as well as staff and equipment, is needed for the project.

▶ **A compound subject (more than one subject) joined by *and* requires a
   plural verb.**

   Completing the form and mailing it promptly are important.
   Becky and Suzie have resigned over this matter.

▶ **A compound subject joined by *or* or *nor* takes a singular verb.**

   The chairman or the president is willing to discuss the financial goals for
   the year.

▶ **In either/or and neither/nor constructions, the verb agrees with the
   nearest subject.**

   Either the employer or the employees are going to pay the tax.
   Neither the buyers nor the sales manager is in favor of the system.

PROOFREADING FOR GRAMMATICAL ERRORS (continued)

► Use a singular verb after these subjects: *each, each one, every, everyone, everybody, either, neither, nobody, no one, anyone, anybody, another, one, somebody, someone,* and *much.*

Everyone is required to register in order to vote.
Much remains to be done.

► Use a plural verb after these subjects: *both, few, many, others,* and *several.*

Both maps are out of print.
Many were invited, but few were able to participate.

► Collective nouns:

If the group is acting as a unit, use a singular verb.

The Board of Directors meets on Wednesday.
The staff supports the move.

If the members of the group are acting separately, use a plural verb.

The council are divided about the school bond issue.
The majority are unwilling to contribute to the office party.

✍ EXERCISE FIVE—AGREEMENT

Proofread for subject–verb agreement. Circle the correct answer for each of the following. See page 86 for answers.

1. Either coffee or tea (is, are) served at the refreshment breaks.

2. The greatest nuisance (is, are) the refunds we have to make.

3. Each of the supervisors (needs, need) a planning calendar.

4. The committee (has, have) agreed to submit the report next week.

5. Neither the president nor the membership (was, were) in favor of meeting weekly.

6. Either May or June (is, are) a good time for the regional conference.

7. This study, as well as many earlier studies, (shows, show) that turnover is declining steadily.

8. A system of lines (extends, extend) horizontally to form a grid.

9. The panel, consisting of outstanding representatives from private industry and government, (has agreed, have agreed) to accept questions on the report.

10. Everybody in the meeting (was, were) becoming restless as the discussion continued.

KNOW YOUR PRONOUNS

Pronouns are one of the eight parts of speech; they take the place of nouns in sentences. There are three case forms of pronouns. They are (1) nominative, (2) objective, and (3) possessive.

Nominative pronouns function as the subjects in sentences. They are the "naming" pronouns. Objective pronouns function as objects in sentences or as objects of prepositions. Possessive pronouns show ownership. Unlike other possessive words, possessive pronouns are never formed with an apostrophe.

Review this chart of pronoun cases.

Nominative *Subjects*	I	he	she	we	they	who	you	it
Objective *Objects*	me	him	her	us	them	whom	you	it
Possessive *Ownership*	my mine	his	her hers	our ours	their theirs	whose	your yours	its

EXAMPLES: Susan and I attended the banquet with Bill and him.

We officers will complete the drill today.

It was their flipchart and my markers that were left in the room.

You and I must meet at 3 p.m. to discuss the financials with them.

NOUN/PRONOUN AGREEMENT GUIDELINES AHEAD . . .

Guidelines for Noun/Pronoun Agreement

► **A noun and its pronoun must agree in person, number, and gender, whether they act as subject, object, or possessor.**

I must stand by *my* client, just as *you* must stand by *yours.*

Nancy wants to know whether *her* proposal has been accepted.

Roger said that *he* could do the project alone.

The grand *jury* has completed *its* investigation.

► **Use a plural pronoun when the antecedent (the word or phrase to which the pronoun refers) consists of two nouns joined by *and*.**

Harriet and Claire have submitted *their* proposals.

► **Use a singular pronoun when the antecedent consists of two *singular* nouns joined by *or* or *nor*.**

Either Bill or Fred will have to give up *his* office.

► **Use a plural pronoun when the antecedent consists of two *plural* nouns joined by *or* or *nor*.**

Neither the *Cramers* nor the *Leonards* can bring *their* camera.

► **When a pronoun refers to nouns joined by *or, nor, either/or,* or *neither/nor* and one of the nouns is plural, make the pronoun match the closest noun.**

Neither Mr. Polk nor his employees have reached *their* goal.

THE TOUGH ISSUES

Who or Whom? That is the Question.

Proofreaders everywhere struggle with this issue. When you keep these rules in mind, you'll know the correct word to choose.

▶ Use *who* and *whoever* whenever you could substitute *he, she, they, I,* or *we* in the *who* clause.

Who is waiting? (*She* is waiting.)

Who did they say was chosen? (Did they say *he* was chosen?)

The job goes to *whoever* answers the ad first. (*He* answers the ad first.)

> *Whenever who/whom is found in the middle of a sentence,*
>
> *cover all words before who/whom and substitute.*

▶ Use *whom* and *whomever* whenever you could substitute *him, her, them, me,* or *us* as the object of a verb or the object of a preposition in the *whom* clause.

Whom did you ask to pick up the order? (Did you ask *him* to pick up the order?)

Whom did you say you wanted to see? (Did you say you wanted to see *her*?)

The job goes to *whomever* you call first. (You call *him* first.)

I/Me/Myself—What's a Writer To Use?

► **"I" is a nominative pronoun and is used as a subject of a sentence.**

    EXAMPLE: *I* suggest we schedule the meeting for next Thursday. ("I" is the subject of the sentence.)

► **"Me" is an objective-case pronoun and is used as an object of a verb or an object of a prepositional phrase.**

    EXAMPLE: The report was distributed to Lauree and *me*. (In this sentence "me" is the object of the prepositional phrase "to Lauree and me." You would not write, "The report was distributed to Lauree and I."

                  Lauree notified *me* that the report had been copied and distributed to all staff members. (Here the word "me" is the object of the verb "notified." Lauree notified who? Me, not I.)

► **Use "myself" only for emphasis such as "I signed up for it myself" or as a reflexive form of the personal pronoun as in "I myself am going."**

> *A simple rule to follow: Avoid writing "myself."*

Common Mistakes:

• Debra and myself worked on the budget.
(Debra and *I* worked on the budget.)

• Tom is attending the conference with Dennis and myself.
(Tom is attending the conference with Dennis and *me*.)

> ### *Quick Tip*
>
> *With a compound subject or object—cover the proper noun to verify the pronoun. In the above examples, cover Debra and Dennis; then read the sentence aloud to verify accuracy.*

THE TOUGH ISSUES (continued)

Gender Considerations

The issue of sexist writing may seem insignificant, but it's not. As a proofreader, you need to be aware of the guidelines that will help you use gender-neutral language in your business correspondence.

► **Use gender-neutral terms whenever possible.**

Instead of:	*Use:*
mankind	humankind
mothering	parenting
fireman	fire fighter
policeman	police officer
to man (verb)	to operate; to staff
workmen's compensation	worker's compensation

► **To avoid gender-specific pronouns, change the wording in a sentence from singular to plural.**

From:	Each supervisor must submit his proposal.
To:	Supervisors must submit their proposals.

► **Avoid "s/he," "he/she," and "his/her." They sound and look awkward. Instead, use "he or she" and "his or her."**

► **Sometimes gender-specific pronouns can simply be eliminated, as in these examples:**

Change:	Each operator worked on his machine.
To:	Each operator worked on a machine.

Change:	The candidate must send his loan application by Friday.
To:	The candidate must send a loan application by Friday.

or

Please send your loan application by Friday.

Let's Practice

Let's review our three tough grammar issues—who/whom, I/me/myself, and sexist language. Rewrite the first sentence, and choose the correct answer in the following sentences.

1. Each director must meet with his staff to discuss each of his performance appraisals.

_____

_____

2. Bradley and (I, me, myself) will make our presentation to the Pentagon staff this afternoon.

3. I will speak to (whoever, whomever) answers the telephone.

4. (Who/Whom) did you verify the budget figures with before the planning session?

5. Be sure to submit all travel expenses to either Kate or (I, me, myself).

Answers:
1. Directors must meet with each staff member to discuss performance appraisals.
2. I
3. whoever
4. Whom
5. me

DANGLING AND MISPLACED MODIFIERS

A modifier is a word or group of words that describes something. It must be placed in the sentence so that the intended meaning is clear to the reader.

Dangling Modifiers

When a modifier does not refer to anything in the sentence, it is called a *dangling modifier.* To correct a dangling modifier, add words to make the meaning clear.

Instead of: While working on the manuscript, the word processor continually broke down.

Write: While I was working on the manuscript, the word processor continually broke down.

Instead of: Having read the instructions carefully, my video tape recorder was easily assembled.

Write: Having read the instructions carefully, I was able to assemble my video tape recorder easily.

Misplaced Modifiers

When a modifier is not close to the word it modifies, it can produce an ambiguous or humorous result. To correct the problem, move the modifier.

Instead of: The manager issued a memory typewriter to the assistant with removable storage.

Write: The manager issued a memory typewriter with removable storage to the assistant.

Instead of: Only we paid for the terminal, not the software program.

Write: We paid only for the terminal, not the software program.

Let's Practice

Rewrite the following sentences to eliminate dangling or misplaced modifiers.

1. To meet the deadline, all mailings have to be completed by 4 p.m.

_____

_____

2. The procedures manual was a welcome sight to Arthur lying on the desk.

_____

_____

Answers:
1. To meet the deadline, you need to complete all mailings by 4 p.m.
2. The procedures manual, lying on the desk, was a welcome sight to Arthur.

✍ EXERCISE SIX—AGREEMENT AND PRONOUNS

Proofread this memo, and correct the subject/verb agreement, sexist language, and pronoun mistakes. See Page 87 for answers.

To: All Department Supervisors
From: Erika Chandler, CEO

The management team of Sulsen Designs have decided to implement a new system throughout the organization: Cross-Functional Work Teams. This innovative approach to cooperative management will be explained and presented in detail at an upcoming meeting for supervisors.

Each supervisor is expected to attend the meeting and make a presentation to his department. Cross-functional work teams are necessary because commercial clients are requiring more personalized service, and residential clients demands more diversity.

A consulting team has been working with senior management and I to facilitate the transition to this exciting program. If you have any questions before the meeting, please address them to Scooter Mijer, Director of Human Resources, or myself. We will speak to whomever has specific, logistical concerns.

PROOFREADING FOR PUNCTUATION ERRORS

Reading maketh a full man;
conference a ready man;
and writing an exact man.

—Francis Bacon, Lord Chancellor of England
(Superstition)

Did your English teacher ever tell you, "Put a comma wherever you would take a breath"? Have you ever not used a semicolon because you weren't sure where to place it? When you get to the end of a sentence, have you hesitated, wondering whether the period goes inside or outside the closing quotation mark?

If the use of punctuation marks seems arbitrary, think again! There is a method to the madness, and once again help is on the way!

Study this section on proofreading for punctuation errors. You'll find that it will work as a mini-reference guide.

✓ **COMMAS**

✓ **SEMICOLONS**

✓ **COLONS**

✓ **APOSTROPHES**

✓ **PARENTHESES**

✓ **DASHES**

✓ **QUOTATION MARKS**

COMMAS ,

A comma:

- is the most widely used punctuation mark
- is the most problematic because its uses vary so much (it's both overused and underused!)
- indicates a brief pause for the reader
- is always used *within* the sentence (never at the beginning or the end)
- serves several purposes: to separate, to introduce, to enclose

► **Use a comma to separate a series of words or group of words. Place a comma before the *and* preceding the last item.**

EXAMPLES: We arrived at the airport, waited in line, checked our baggage, and walked down the concourse to our plane.

I placed the order for magazines, newspapers, journals, and newsletters.

► **Use a comma after an introductory word, phrase, or clause.**

EXAMPLES: She needed only one thing, confidence.

Yes, the Marketing Department will be attending the summer conference.

► **Use a comma after the calendar year if it follows the month and day. A comma is not needed following the month and year.**

EXAMPLES: She will arrive on September 22, 1995, for the training session.

She will arrive in September 1995 for the training session.

► **Use a comma to separate two or more adjectives that describe a noun. (Reminder: The comma is taking the place of the word *and*.)**

EXAMPLES: The applicant was professional, knowledgeable, and experienced in the area of accounting.

Arizona is a hot, dry state.

► **Use commas to enclose the name of anyone you are writing directly to when the name is used in the body of your document.**

EXAMPLES: Thank you, Penny, for responding so quickly to my request.

I'm counting on you to get the order processed this week, Ms. Sinclair.

► **Use commas to enclose parenthetical words, phrases, or clauses.**

EXAMPLES: The additional supply order, however, will not be shipped until early tomorrow.

Ms. Nell Temple, our new association chapter president, will be introduced at our next monthly meeting.

► **Use a comma to separate two independent clauses joined by a conjunction. Memory tip: "BOYS FAN" (*But, Or, Yet, So, For, And, Nor*).**

EXAMPLES: There are two job openings for a person with sales experience, and I know you'll get one of them!

We would like to have our human resources staff attend the national conference, but we cannot afford the high costs.

Hyphen Help

A common question for many of our readers involves the correct use of the hyphen. You may wonder which words are hyphenated and which are not. Hyphenation rules are continually changing, so the best advice is to check a dictionary or word division guide.

SEMICOLONS ;

The semicolon:

- is a mark used for separation or division only
- functions as a stronger break than a comma
- is never used to end a sentence

► **Use a semicolon to separate two or more independent clauses related in meaning and not joined with a conjunction.**

EXAMPLES: Operations tripled productivity in the first quarter; finance doubled productivity.

The new employee was perfectly suited for his new job in the customer service department; he learned the systems and procedures in less than a month.

► **Use a semicolon to separate equal parts of a sentence when commas would be confusing.**

EXAMPLES: The officers of the union are John Romero, president; Susan Greenberg, vice president; Becky O'Rourke, treasurer; James Jackson, secretary; and Jan Johnson, historian.

► **Use a semicolon to separate two independent clauses joined by a transitional expression (consequently, nevertheless, however, therefore). Follow this easy formula:**

independent clause–semicolon–transitional expression–comma–independent clause

EXAMPLES: Ruth was terrific in dealing with difficult customers by phone; consequently, we forwarded all the tough calls to her.

He worked overtime to solve the computer difficulties; in fact, he rarely got home before 9 p.m. each night.

COLONS :

A colon:

- is a mark of expectation or addition
- signals to the reader that there's more to come
- introduces lists and enumerations

► **Use a colon after a salutation in a business letter.**

EXAMPLE: Dear Ms. Norton:

► **Use a colon to separate a title from a subtitle in a book.**

EXAMPLE: *The Meeting Planning Reference Source: Hospitality in the 1990s*

► **Use a colon to introduce lists.**

EXAMPLE: Among the cities represented were the following: Littleton, Northglenn, Aurora, Denver, and Boulder.

► **Use a colon to separate hours and minutes in time.**

EXAMPLE: 1:30 p.m.   7:17 a.m.

APOSTROPHES ,

An apostrophe:

- functions as a punctuation mark and a spelling symbol
- indicates omission of letter(s)
- forms possessives
- forms plurals

► **Use an apostrophe where a letter or letters have been omitted.**

EXAMPLES: can't (cannot)   couldn't (could not)   it's (it is)

► **Use an apostrophe where a figure or figures have been omitted.**

EXAMPLES: Class of '76 (1976)   late in '90 (1990)

► **Use an apostrophe to show plurals for single letters.**

EXAMPLES: dot your *i's*
watch your *p's* and *q's*

► **Use an apostrophe to show possession (ownership).**

EXAMPLES:	*SINGULAR*	*PLURAL*
Any word not ending in "s"	's	's
Any word ending in "s"	'*	'

---

*An exception is a singular word ending in "s" that creates an extra syllable for pronunciation; in that case, form possession by adding " 's."

boss's   Ms. Jones's

Let's Practice

Add possession to each of these phrases.

1. Grant_____ briefcase

2. The shrubs _____ leaves

3. The witness _____ testimony

4. Investors _____ objectives

5. Congress _____ plans

6. The judges _____ rulings

7. The twins _____ room

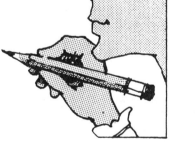

Answers:
1. Grant's (Grant is singular and doesn't end in "s")
2. shrubs' (shrubs is plural and ends in "s")
3. witness's (witness is singular, ends in "s," but when changed to possessive is pronounced with an added syllable)
4. Investors' (Investors is plural and ends in "s")
5. Congress's (Congress is a collective noun [singular], ends in "s," but when changed to possessive is pronounced with an added syllable)
6. judges' (judges is plural and ends in "s")
7. twins' (twins is plural and ends in "s")

PARENTHESES ( )

Parentheses:

- are used to enclose nonessential material
- signal "by the way" to the reader
- shouldn't be overused

► **Use parentheses to enclose material connected with its surrounding text.**

EXAMPLES: The illustration (see page 34) is very important.

Marion doesn't feel (and why should she) that she should work overtime on the project by herself.

DASHES –

A dash:

- is an emphatic mark
- indicates a sudden interruption in thought
- is two strokes of the hyphen key on a typewriter
- has no space before or after it
- should not be overused

▶ **Use a dash to show emphasis.**

EXAMPLE: Power, money, fame—these were her aspirations in life.

QUOTATION MARKS " "

Quotation marks:

- enclose words, phrases, clauses, sentences, or paragraphs
- indicate *repeating* or *copying* what someone has said or written

► **Use quotation marks to show the exact words of a person being quoted.**

EXAMPLE: I asked the interviewer, "What will the starting salary be?"

► **Use quotation marks to set off technical terms or special expressions.**

EXAMPLES: New York is often called "The Big Apple."
Behind his back, we called our new manager "The Big Cheese."

► **Periods and commas are placed inside the closing quotation mark.**

EXAMPLE: "I wanted," she said, "to finish this meeting on time."

► **Colons and semicolons are placed outside the closing quotation mark.**

EXAMPLE: The following animals are considered "marsupials": kangaroo, koala, and opossum.

► **Question marks and exclamation points can be placed inside or outside the closing quotation mark.**

EXAMPLES: "How are you?" I asked. (*The question mark is placed inside the closing quotation mark because the entire quoted material—How are you—is a question.*)

Have you read the report, "Successful Start-Up Businesses"? (*The question mark is placed outside the closing quotation mark because the entire sentence is a question.*)

✍ EXERCISE SEVEN—PUNCTUATION ERRORS

It's that time again! Read the following document, and insert the appropriate punctuation marks. See page 88 for answers.

Are you ready to put your punctuation knowledge to the test Read through this document once before making any proofreaders marks Then go back and put in any necessary punctuation marks As you can already tell there are no punctuation marks at all you get to test your proofreading for punctuation errors Have fun

Punctuation marks have often been compared to road signs They direct the reader through the document Imagine if you were driving through your citys streets and there were no traffic signs chaos would result Its important to use the appropriate signs and then your reader will quickly and efficiently be able to read and comprehend your document Dont you find it rather difficult reading this exercise with no punctuation marks

The punctuation marks youll use most frequently are as follows period comma semicolon parentheses question mark apostrophe and quotation marks Did I leave any out Look over your document one more time and make sure youve caught all the errors

PROOFREADING FOR SPELLING ERRORS

"It's an awfully unimaginative person who can think of only one way to spell a word."

—Mark Twain

Spelling Suggestions

Spelling may sound basic, but to a proofreader, it's critical. Misspelled words in correspondence present your message in a negative way and can cause misunderstanding in your communication. If you struggle with spelling, consider these tips:

- Develop the habit of spelling every word correctly. (Becoming a good speller is a matter of attitude!)

- When in doubt, consult a spelling dictionary, a dictionary, a thesaurus, or a style guide.

- Pronounce words slowly to make sure you are not missing any syllables.

- Use a spell-check software program.

- Study common spelling rules.

- Study lists of frequently misspelled words, and practice writing them correctly.

- Pay more attention to words that have five or more letters.

- Watch for words that are *always* spelled as one word: cannot, nobody, somebody, somewhat, wherever, and worthwhile.

- Watch for words that are *always* spelled as two words: a lot, in spite, all right (alright with one "l" is acceptable too).

- To catch spelling errors, read copy from right to left or from bottom to top.

- To improve your accuracy in spelling, read aloud or touch each word.

- When you are not sure of a word, ask the writer.

- As you read, study correctly spelled words.

200 Frequently Misspelled Words

a lot	Des Moines	itinerary	queue
absence	descendant	jeopardy	receipt
accidentally	dilemma	judgment	recipient
accommodate	disappoint	knowledge	recognize
accompanying	dissimilar	ledger	reference
achievement	dissipate	leisure	Renaissance
acquaintance	dossier	license	renowned
acquiesce	ecstasy	lien	rescind
admissible	eighth	lieutenant	resistance
adolescent	eligible	lightning	rhapsody
Albuquerque	embarrass	likable	rhetorical
all right	emphasize	lose	rhythm
amateur	entrepreneur	maintenance	salable
analyze	enumerate	maneuver	satellite
annihilate	environment	mediocre	scissors
anoint	exaggerate	mileage	seize
antiquated	exhaustible	miniature	separate
apparent	exhibition	mortgage	siege
appropriate	exhilarate	movable	simultaneous
assistance	exonerate	necessary	sizable
awkward	exorbitant	nickel	souvenir
bachelor	extraordinary	ninety	subpoena
bankruptcy	eyeing	ninth	subtly
battalion	facsimile	noticeable	superintendent
beneficiary	familiar	nuclear	supersede
benefited	fascinating	obsolescent	surprise
biased	financier	occasionally	susceptible
buoyant	foreign	occurrence	technique
bureaucracy	forfeit	omission	temperament
calendar	fulfill	opinion	theater
canceled	gauge	pamphlet	thoroughly
cancellation	glamour	parallel	threshold
Caribbean	grammar	pastime	tragedy
catalyst	guarantee	permissible	transferred
changeable	guardian	perseverance	tyranny
Cincinnati	harass	persistent	unanimous
coincidence	height	persuade	unforgettable
colonel	hemorrhage	phenomenal	unique
commitment	hindrance	Pittsburgh	unwieldy
connoisseur	hygiene	plausible	usable
conscientious	hypocrisy	preceding	utilization
conscious	illogical	presumptuous	vacillate
consensus	impasse	privilege	vacuum
controlled	inadvertent	programmed	volume
criticism	incidentally	promissory	Wednesday
debtor	indispensable	pronunciation	weird
deceive	innocuous	pseudonym	wholly
deductible	innuendo	psychiatric	wield
defendant	irrelevant	quantity	woeful
dependent	irresistible	questionnaire	yield

SPELLING TIP

You may ask, "Why should I bother to learn spelling rules? I'm an adult, and the days of spelling tests are long gone. Anyway, I have a computer with a spell-checker."

It's tough to disagree with that argument! We would, however, argue that the better speller you are, the more time you'll save and the more mistakes you'll catch. When your spelling improves, your proofreading improves.

So what do you do now? Study ten words each week and test yourself on Friday? Forget it. We have a solution that's easier.

Identify the five words related to your company, job, or industry that you can't spell correctly. Write them down on a sticky note or index card. Post them at work near your computer, desk blotter, or calendar. Post them at home near your mirror or refrigerator. Every time you glance at the words, repeat the spelling of one or two of them in your mind. I-N-C-O-N-V-E-N-I-E-N-C-E Inconvenience. You'll be amazed at how soon you can quickly and accurately improve your spelling!

Abbreviations

Spell out an abbreviation the first time it is used, and follow it with the abbreviation: American Management Association (AMA). Any additional references can be abbreviated.

Word Search Game

Here's another word search game to test your skill at finding words "disguised" in text. All these words are related to punctuation. Enjoy yourself!

```
H  I  Q  F  W  N  Z  D  B  T  R  N  S  Y
S  U  U  A  N  F  L  P  X  H  E  J  K  N
K  A  P  O  S  T  R  O  P  H  E  N  C  O
R  D  K  Y  D  S  R  C  P  G  F  O  X  L
A  H  O  S  J  T  L  Y  Z  D  M  L  V  O
M  C  F  I  S  K  H  S  D  M  D  P  S  C
N  X  Z  O  R  Y  F  Z  A  W  A  Z  D  I
O  H  P  A  R  E  N  T  H  E  S  E  S  M
I  A  G  D  F  C  P  T  G  Q  H  H  K  E
T  M  W  Q  K  Y  V  X  C  Z  G  C  L  S
S  K  R  A  M  N  O  I  T  A  T  O  U  Q
E  J  L  S  I  H  C  J  F  B  G  L  C  T
U  D  P  F  E  L  Q  S  T  V  H  O  S  Y
Q  U  E  S  S  N  B  E  J  M  O  N  P  R
```

1. QUOTATION MARKS	**6.** PERIOD	
2. COLON	**7.** APOSTROPHE	
3. QUESTION MARKS	**8.** COMMA	
4. PARENTHESES	**9.** HYPHEN	
5. DASH	**10.** SEMICOLON	

PROOFREADING FOR USAGE ERRORS

"Upgrading your communications skills is the surest way to open the door to a job or to jumpstart a stalled career."

—Harvey B. Mackay, author

A major challenge of the English language is that many words sound alike but have different meanings or spellings. To be an expert proofreader, you need to be able to distinguish between words that sound alike or are spelled similarly, so that you will be able to detect and correct errors in their usage.

The meaning and spelling of the following pairs are commonly confused:

accept, except
    accept—*v.* to receive, to take
    except—*prep.* excluding, omitting

advice, advise
    advice—*n.* recommendation, opinion
    advise—*v.* to counsel

affect, effect
    affect—*v.* to influence
    effect—*n.* an outcome or result
            v. to cause to happen

all ready, already
    all ready—*adj. phrase,* all prepared
    already—*adv.* by or before this time

among, between
    among—*prep.* used for more than two persons or things
    between—*prep.* used with two persons or things

assure, ensure, insure
    assure—*v.* to make confident
    ensure—*v.* to make certain something happens
    insure—*v.* to buy insurance

capital, capitol
    capital—*n.* seat of government; wealth
    capitol—*n.* government building

cite, sight, site
    cite—*v.* to quote or state
    sight—*n.* scene, view; *v.* to see
    site—*n.* location

complement, compliment
    complement—*n.* something that completes
              v. to complete or make perfect
    compliment—*n.* recognition, flattering remark
              v. to praise

consul, council, counsel
    consul—*n.* foreign embassy official
    council—*n.* assembly, governing body
    counsel—*v.* to give advice, advise
           n. legal advisor; advice

continual, continuous
    continual—*adj.* action that occurs at frequent intervals
    continuous—*adj.* action that occurs without pauses

criteria, criterion
    criteria—*n.* standards of judgment or criticism
    criterion—*n.* singular form of criteria

disinterested, uninterested
    disinterested—*adj.* impartial, showing no preferences or prejudice
    uninterested—*adj.* bored or lacking interest

eager, anxious
    eager—*adj.* fervent, enthusiastic
    anxious—*adj.* full of anxiety or worry due to apprehension

emigrate, immigrate
    emigrate—*v.* to leave one country or region to settle in another
    immigrate—*v.* to come to a country of which one is not a native to live

PROOFREADING FOR USAGE ERRORS
(continued)

farther, further
> farther—*adv.* refers to physical distance
> further—*adv.* refers to degree or extent

fewer, less
> fewer—*adj.* used for individual units, numbers
> less—*adj.* used for quantities

imply, infer
> imply—*v.* to suggest
> infer—*v.* to deduce from evidence

its, it's
> its—*adj.* possessive form of it
> it's—*contraction* of it is and it has

lay, lie
> lay—*v.* to put or place something
> lie—*v.* to rest or recline

principal, principle
> principal—*n.* main, chief; superintendent
> principle—*n.* rule, standard, general truth

set, sit
> set—*v.* to put or place something
> sit—*v.* to assume an upright position

stationary, stationery
> stationary—*adj.* fixed in one position
> stationery—*n.* paper for writing

than, then
> than—*conj.* after a comparison; when
> then—*adv.* next; in that case

their, there, they're
> their—*adj.* possessive form of they
> there—*adv.* at that place
> they're—*contraction* of they are

✍ EXERCISE EIGHT—USAGE ERRORS

Circle the appropriate word. See pages 89–90 for answers.

1. We are (anxious, eager) to participate in the sales training program.

2. The service representative (assured, ensured, insured) the customer that the shipment would arrive on schedule.

3. There is a conflict (among, between) operations and marketing.

4. The reorganization will (affect, effect) the home office as well as the regional offices.

5. When you are finished with the reports, please (lay, lie) them on my desk.

6. You may be able to provide (consul, council, counsel) to Marie since you have attended the officers' meetings in the past.

7. Do you (imply, infer) by your complaints that you don't want to use the new computer software program?

8. The Sales Department has set its goals (farther, further) than the Marketing Department.

9. The computer (continually, continuously) breaks down.

10. I suggest that you (accept, except) the job offer from the West Coast.

11. (Its, It's) going to take four weeks for the new equipment to arrive.

12. The committee decided it will need more (capital, capitol) to finance the new product line.

13. To receive a higher rating on your next performance evaluation, you will need to make (fewer, less) mistakes in your work.

14. I no sooner began my briefing (than, then) Fred interrupted me.

15. Follow this (advice, advise): get to work on time.

16. We are (all ready, already) to begin work on the Fullerton project.

17. His humor is the perfect (complement, compliment) to my seriousness.

EXERCISE EIGHT (continued)

18. Our nonprofit organization just received a large endowment from its (principal, principle) benefactor.

19. The next time you order (stationary, stationery) for our office, use the telephone by the (stationary, stationery) terminal.

20. If you disagree with the proposal, be sure to (cite, site, sight) your reasons.

21. Ask the accountants to (set, sit) their materials in the next office.

22. As a (disinterested, uninterested) member, she can give an objective decision.

23. Managers must use (their, there, they're) judgment when disciplining employees.

24. Remember that you (emigrate, immigrate) from a country and (emigrate, immigrate) into a country.

25. Service, not price, is the main (criteria, criterion) we use when we make our purchasing decisions.

PROOFREADING FOR CAPITALIZATION ERRORS

"The person who was not content to do small things well would leave great things undone."

—Ellen Glasgow (*Voice of the People*)

Why do we capitalize words? The answer is simple: to give words distinction, emphasis, and importance. Yet confusion abounds regarding capitalization rules. When do you capitalize a word and when do you not capitalize a word? If you capitalize too many words, none stand out. On the other hand, if you don't capitalize a word, its importance goes unrecognized. What a dilemma!

Whatever your thoughts, know that the current trend in organizations is to go light—capitalize only when and where it is appropriate to give emphasis, distinction, and importance. If your organization is specialized and you have your own style guide, then follow it. If not, follow the rules on the following pages.

CAPITALIZATION AT A GLANCE

First word of a sentence, question, or direct quotation	Rest everyday. What time is it? The memo read, "Follow these guidelines immediately."
First word of each item in a displayed list or outline	Please order the following supplies: Stationery Envelopes Business cards
Proper names	Valli Daniels Mississippi River Statue of Liberty
Languages, religions, races, and peoples	English, Catholic, Japanese
Descriptive names or nicknames	the First Lady
Words derived from proper names	Californian, Austinite
Academic degrees following a personal name whether abbreviated or written in full	James Doluisio, Ph.D. Tina Allen, Master of Social Sciences
Course titles	Anthropology 101 Physics 2
Days of the week	Sunday, Monday
Months	January, February
Holidays, holy days	Christmas, Hanukkah
Periods, events in history	Reformation, War of 1812

Special events	Rose Parade
Official documents	Bill of Rights
Formal epithets	Alexander the Great
Planets, heavenly bodies	Mars, Earth, the Milky Way
Continents	Africa, Australia
Streets, roads, highways	Main Street, U.S. 101
States and cities	Maryland, Fort Wayne
Sections of a country or continent	the Southwest the Middle East
Landforms	Mojave Desert, Rocky Mountains
Bodies of water	Lake Michigan, Pacific Ocean
Public areas	Yellowstone National Park
Buildings, organizations, institutions	Marriott Hotel Girl Scouts of America Chicago Public Library
Family members and specific classes	Mom, Dad, Grandpa, Class of '70

CAPITALIZATION (continued)

Titles

▶ Capitalize all official titles of honor and respect when they *precede* personal names.

    EXAMPLES: Ms. Teresa Goodwin
                 President James Salzman
                 Reverend Kenneth Smith

▶ Do not capitalize such titles when the personal name that follows is in apposition and is set off by commas.

    EXAMPLES: Yesterday the president, Janet Rumlow, presented the revised budget.

                           or

                 President Janet Rumlow presented the revised budget.

▶ In general, do not capitalize titles of honor and respect when they *follow* a personal name or are used in *place* of a personal name.

    EXAMPLES: Janet Rumlow, president of Rumlow Publications, will be retiring next year. During her ten years as president, the company grew by 60 percent.

Note: Exceptions are made for important officials and dignitaries.

▶ Capitalize organizational names when they refer to specific departments or groups within the originator's own organization. Do not use capitals when referring to a department or group in another organization.

    EXAMPLES: Joann works in the Creative Department.
                 Does David represent their sales department?

Names of Places

▶ Capitalize the *city* only when it is part of the corporate name of the city or part of an imaginative name.

    EXAMPLES: New York City
                 But: The city of New Orleans
                 the Windy City (Chicago)

▶ Capitalize *state* only when it follows the name of a state or is part of an imaginative name.

EXAMPLES: The state of Texas is known as the Lone Star State.
New York State is called the Empire State.

Points of the Compass

▶ Capitalize *north, south, east, west,* and derivative words when they designate definite regions or are part of a proper name.

EXAMPLES: in the North
back East
the Deep South
the West Coast

▶ Do not capitalize these words when they merely indicate direction or general location.

EXAMPLE: Drive west on I-70 and then north on Highway 135.

Seasons

▶ Do not capitalize the seasons of the year unless they are portrayed as persons.

EXAMPLES: fall meeting
spring conference
Old Man Winter

Trade Names

▶ Capitalize the trade names of manufactured products, but lowercase the words following a trade name that are not part of the name.

EXAMPLES: Ivory soap
General Electric refrigerator
Dell computer
Canon copier

CAPITALIZATION (continued)

Titles of Literary Works, Artistic Works, and Headings

▶ **Capitalize all words with *five or more* letters. Also capitalize words with fewer than five letters except:**

Articles: *the, a, an*
Short conjunctions: *and, as, but, if, or, nor*
Short prepositions: *at, by, for, in, of, off, on, out, to, up, with*
The infinitive: *to*

Quick Tip

Even articles, short conjunctions, short prepositions, and the infinitive "to" should be capitalized when they are the first and last words of a title.

"The Star-Spangled Banner"
Fiddler on the Roof
"How to Deal with Difficult People"
Drums Along the Mohawk
To Kill a Mockingbird

✍ EXERCISE NINE—CAPITALIZATION

Read the following letter, and capitalize the appropriate words. See page 91 for answers.

senator grant jones
state capitol
6421 sacramento street, n.w.
sacramento, california 62111

dear senator jones:

this letter is to inform you of the opposition of the california retailers association to senate bill 1246.

as you are aware, we represent the majority of all retail businesses in california. some of our more prominent members are samson's, short drug stores, capital camera, derby corporation, and all divisions of acme department stores.

our members are concerned with the provision of the bill that would exempt out-of-state mail order firms from a state sales tax. this matter was discussed at our spring legislative conference held in san diego at the hilton hotel. the membership of the association voted unanimously to oppose senate bill 1246 because of this provision.

for example, we are concerned that companies such as austin express and sparrow's computer corporation are able to mail their products into california and not incur any state sales tax. also, this bill does not even address the issue of local sales taxes such as those in west los angeles county.

senator, we appreciate your assistance in this matter and look forward to meeting with you.

sincerely

chuck billkiller
executive vice president
california retailers association

PROOFREADING FOR NUMBER ERRORS

Another question arises when proofreading numbers—when do you use words and when do you use figures or numerals? Do you want the number to stand out in the sentence? If so, use numerals. Do you want the number to be less obtrusive and formal? Use word format. However, since deciding the correct form based on these two suggestions is too subjective, consider these rules for expressing numbers.

Rule #1: Numbers Expressed as Words

EXPRESS AS WORDS	EXAMPLE
Numbers from one to ten	five, seven, nine
Numbers beginning a sentence	Six hundred people attended the conference.
Ordinal numbers expressed in one or two words	In the twenty-first century the company's fiftieth anniversary
Exact or approximate numbers that can be expressed in one or two words	about one-half of the constituents more than three million letters
Smaller of two numbers when used together and one is part of a compound modifier	three 30-pound cartons 25 four-cent stamps
Street names of ten or less and house/building number One	One Park Avenue 1738 Third Street
Ages (unless expressed in years and months)	Jon is turning twenty-two this year. Sophia is 2 years and 6 months old.
Fractions when they occur without a whole number	One-fourth of the shareholders attended.
Time when stated in numbers alone or before o'clock	See you at ten. The meeting begins at two o'clock.
The word *cents* if the amount is less than a dollar	Each notepad costs 75 cents.

Rule #2: Numbers Expressed as Numerals

EXPRESS AS NUMERALS	EXAMPLE
Numbers 11 and above	18, 29, 55, 213
A series of numbers, any of which is over ten	We need to purchase 5 rolls of tape, 8 pens, 15 file folders, and 24 pencils.
Large round numbers followed by the word million or billion	5 million customers 19 billion particles
Ordinal numbers that cannot be expressed in one or two words	Tomorrow is the 120th day of the strike.
Street names over ten and all house/building numbers except One (Can be expressed as cardinal or ordinal numbers)	15 West 22nd Street (or 15 West 22 Street)
Mixed numbers	3 1/2 boxes of computer ribbons
Time when a.m., noon, midnight, and p.m. are used	Gina has a meeting at 9 a.m. and another at 3 p.m.
Dates in business letters *Note: When the day follows the month, express it in cardinal figures (1, 2, 3, etc.). When the day precedes the month or stands alone, express it either in ordinal figures (1st, 2nd, etc.) or in ordinal words (the first, the second).*	May 17, 1999 May 17 17th of May
Dimensions, measures, and weights	8 by 10 feet 5 feet 9 inches
Amounts of money *Note: Decimals and zeroes are not used after even amounts unless they appear with fractional amounts.*	I received a $60 invoice. You can pay $150.00 this month and $135.50 for the next three months.
Percentages and decimals	10 percent 665.752394

✍ EXERCISE TEN—NUMBERS

What changes would you make in the following memo? See page 92 for answers.

To: Tony R. Sifuentes
From: Carol E. Fisher
Subject: Formal Disciplinary Hearings Scheduled for July 10th–13th

The agency's calendar for July includes the dates of July 10th, 11th, 12th, and 13th for formal disciplinary hearings. Because of the length of time of hearings each day (8:00 a.m.–6:00 p.m.), we are having problems securing hotel space for the hearings. Most of the hotels we have contacted will only commit the meeting space from 9:00 a.m.–5:00 p.m.

Yesterday my administrative assistant contacted the Joe C. Thompson Conference Center, 4455 3rd Street in Austin to determine whether it had suitable space available for July 10th–13th. She indicated that they had a meeting room one hundred fifty feet by fifty feet that is available. There is also no restriction on time limit for use of the room if we conclude the hearings by 7:00 p.m. each day.

The 1 problem I see is that eighty students from the University of Houston College of Pharmacy may want to attend 2 days of the hearings. Since this room can accommodate only 30-odd members of the class, I suggest we videotape the hearings. The other fifty can view the selected hearings at a later date.

Since the agency does not own the equipment to videotape the proceedings, I would suggest that we contract for this service. 4 vendors are available, but 2 of the 4 bids look the most attractive. Audio-Visual Productions has quoted $350 for 1 eight-hour hearing, and Sound Systems has quoted $349.50. Each requires 1/4 of the total amount as a deposit.

Since time is running short, please contact me by Friday, the 15th of May, so that I can brief you on the specific cases that will be heard in July. If you need to discuss this matter with me on May 6th or 7th, I will be in Washington, D.C. at the Fairmont Hotel, 2 Lexington Avenue, 202/961-3500.

SECTION

III

Summary

PROOFREADER'S POST TEST

Wow! You've successfully made it through the *Powerful Proofreading Skills* book. We've examined proofreading tips and techniques in the areas of grammar, punctuation, spelling, usage, capitalization, and numbers. Are you ready to combine all the information you've learned?

Correct the Proofreader's Post Test letter using the appropriate proofreaders' marks. Hopefully, you'll never see a real letter with this many mistakes. We wanted you to have an opportunity to incorporate all your knowledge and skill.

Your goal is 100 percent accuracy. Check back in the book to review any issue you may be unsure of. Good luck! See page 93 for answers.

Dear Proofreader,

Congratulations! youve completed the powerful proofreading skills book. are you ready to put your new or refreshed skills to the test. Here we go.

As you may already k now communication skills are critical for success in the business world your written and verbal communication skills are a representation of *you* on a daily basis. A promotion or salary increase may be tied to your ability to be accurate and efficient at your workplace.

Lets look back at what youve learned. your workbook covered the following topics proofreading tips and strategies proofreaders marks grammar punctuation capitalization numbers vs. words spelling and usage. Wow! Thats alot of material to cover in just one da y. Perhaps some in formation was new to you perhaps some was simpl y a refresher of material you learned years ago.

Your co-workers and supervisor is going to be anxious to see you produce error-free documents. best of success to you in your business correspondance.

CREATE YOUR OWN PROOFREADER'S LIBRARY

The tools you'll need for proofreading success include:

1. A current dictionary

Throw away your high school or college dictionary from years ago. This is one investment worth the cost.

2. A style sheet

Each company and each boss have certain preferences when it comes to style—formats, capitalization, and spacing often vary. You'll want this information at your fingertips, so you can remain consistent and accurate.

3. A copy of *Powerful Proofreading Skills*

A reference guide can be a lifesaver. Keep this book on your desk! Here are some other "Crisp companions" to help with business writing:

- *Technical Writing in the Corporate World*
- *Writing Fitness*
- *Better Business Writing*
- *Easy English*

SECTION

IV

Exercise Answers

PROOFREADER'S PRETEST ANSWERS

Did you score a perfect 100 percent? If not, you might want to review this book.

1. _____**b**_____ is the correct proofreaders' mark to indicate "delete copy."

   a. ≡   b. ℓ   c. ∩   d. ∿

2. _____**a**_____ is the correct proofreaders' mark to indicate "capitalize."

   a. ≡   b. ℓ   c. ∩   d. ∿

3. Underline the letters that should be capitalized in the following sentences:

   <u>t</u>he repair person flew in from the <u>w</u>est <u>c</u>oast to repair our <u>x</u>erox copier.

   <u>s</u>usan <u>j</u>ames, director of the <u>n</u>ew <u>y</u>ork <u>t</u>heatre <u>c</u>ompany, addressed the cast of *the phantom of the opera.*

4. Correctly punctuate the following sentences:

   Mr⊙Lewis was late to the meeting⊙he was on a conference call with an important client⊙

   Ms⊙Solomonson said⸝"Grace⸝I want you to meet with the doctors from San Francisco⸝Austin⸝Denver⸝Chicago⸝and Boston on September 22⸝ 1995."⊙

5. Please circle all misspelled words in the following sentences:

   We (recieved) the (goverment)(questionaire) and immediately returned it.

   The (unanamous) decision was delivered at the (begining) of the meeting by the marketing (commitee)

   Our third quarter (calender) will (accomodate) your (scheduleing) needs (immediatly.)

PROOFREADER'S PRETEST
ANSWERS(continued)

6. Please circle the correct word from each pair in the following sentences:

   There seems to be a conflict (among, between) sales and marketing.

   The (perspective, prospective) clients will fly in tomorrow to meet with our customer service representatives.

   The computer training will (precede, proceed) the actual installation of the Macintosh equipment.

7. *False:* It can be very useful to proofread with a partner.

8. *False:* To distance yourself means to let some time go by after you write a document so that you can see errors more easily.

9. Which sentence is correct? Underline either *a* or *b*.

   a. The company will distribute its annual report tomorrow.
   b. The company will distribute their annual report tomorrow.

   a. Either the computer or the typewriter are to be moved to the adjoining office.
   b. Either the computer or the typewriter is to be moved to the adjoining office.

   a. The box containing all the office supplies is stored in the spare room.
   b. The box containing all the office supplies are stored in the spare room.

10. Please list five ways to overcome the tedium (pain!) of proofreading long documents.

    a. Take breaks.

    b. Rest your eyes every 10 to 15 minutes.

    c. Proofread with a partner.

    d. Change your pace and/or environment.

    e. Eat lightly throughout the day.

✍ EXERCISE ONE—CHARACTER ACCURACY

Are both columns the same now? Did you catch all the mistakes?

PART A—Names and Telephone Numbers

Ms. Hazel Manning-Smith
(303) 321-1667

Ms. Hazel Manning-Smith
(303) 3̶1̶2̶-1667

Dr. Kim Chong
(402) 346-1926

Dr. Kim Ch°ng
(402) 346-1926

Mr. Russell Graham
(208) 722-4547

Russell
Mr. R̶u̶s̶s̶.̶ L. Graham
(208) 7̶7̶2̶-4̶7̶4̶5̶
2

Mrs. F. A. Lewis
(203) 922-8454

r
M̶s. F.A. Lewis
^   ^
(203) 922-8454

Mr. Albert Sanchez
(616) 232-1917

Mr.
^ Albert Sanchez
(6̶6̶1̶) 232-1̶7̶1̶9̶

Miss Grace Bornheim
(316) 477-2332

Miss
M̶s̶. Grace Bornh̶i̶e̶m̶
(316) 4̶4̶7̶-2332
7

Mr. Washington Jones
(701) 932-1112

Mr. Washington Jones
(701) 932-1112   **(correct)**

Ms. C. Anne Solomonson
(503) 576-8931

Ms. ⌐Anne C.⌐ Solomonson
(3̶0̶5̶) 576-8931
503

Miss Ann L. Schatz
(704) 883-3227

Miss
M̶s̶. Ann L. Schatz
(704) 8̶3̶8̶-3227

Dr. Marin Alsop
(402) 728-7866

Dr.
^ Marin A̶.̶ Alsop
(402) 728-7866

PART B—Invoice Numbers, Measurements, and Account Numbers

January 1 and June 28	January 1ʳ and June 28
ACCT. NO. HRS38930T	ACCT. NO. HRS38930T **(correct)**
Invoice # 125-89-RZD	Invoice # 125-98-RZD
24% increase 16% decrease	42% increase 16% decrease
February 27, 1959, at 4:32 a.m.	February 27, 195⁹8, at 4:32 a.m.
5" x 19" and 23' x 44'	5" x 23¹⁹" and 19²³' x 44'
ACCT. NO. (150M) 7224547 P	ACCT. NO. (150ᴹN) 7224547 P
493257.665	493257.665 **(correct)**
13 1/3 boxes/item #78L	13 1/3 boxes/item #U78
31st of December	31st of December **(correct)**

✎ EXERCISE TWO—USING PROOFREADERS' MARKS

Were you able to find and correct all the typos?

The most common error that you—the proofreader—will find is a typographical error. A "typo" occurs when extra letters, spaces, figures, or copy is added or omitted from a document. Another typo results from transposing (reversing) letters or words. (Will you practice your delete stroke now and delete this entire line of text. Thank you.)

You must remember to slow down your reading rate to spot typographical errors. It is tempting to rush through your documents to to save time; however, in the long run, you'll save time and ensure accuracy if you read carefully.

In addition, it is helpful to use a standard set of proofreaders' marks when you are correcting copy. They are time-savers, and they keep your copy "clean." You'll be able to go back and see your original material as well as your corrections!

Look out for those typos and have fun producing error-free copy!

✍ EXERCISE THREE—PROOFREADERS' MARKS REVIEW

Did you match each mark to its meaning?

C 1. STET	A.	∿
I 2. Start a new paragraph	B.	≡
G 3. Close up the space	C.	⋯
F 4. Delete	D.	*lc*
B 5. Capitalize	E.	DS[
J 6. Spell out	F.	⤸
H 7. Insert punctuation	G.	⌒⌣
A 8. Transpose	H.	⊙ ⋏ ⋎
E 9. Double-space	I.	¶
D 10. Lowercase	J.	⬭

✍ EXERCISE FOUR—SENTENCE STRUCTURE

Did you underline the run-on sentences, and double-underline the sentence fragments correctly?

Dear Mr. Grass:

I received your estimate of $1,500 for the landscaping of our property and find it to be acceptable except for the charges for rearranging the flower beds and relocating the sprinkler system we want it to cover the lawn and the flower beds and the surrounding shrubs that border our property and that of our neighbor. We will expect to see you. On July 10 at our house on Jacobson Drive so we can discuss the work in more detail. Please bring your sketches of the layout because we want to see the details of the landscaping including the colors of the flowers and the types of shrubs you plan to plant after we have approved the layout you can then proceed to complete the landscaping. Please give me a call within the next few days because we need to review the flower beds and sprinkler system so that you can explain the estimates relating to these two items they seem to be somewhat excessive considering the size of our property which is not that large. Call me before 3 p.m. On Tuesday and Wednesday I will be available. Looking forward to meeting with you.

Sincerely,

Sam Spruce

86

✍ EXERCISE FIVE—AGREEMENT

The correct answers for subject–verb agreement are as follows:

1. Either coffee or tea (**is** are) served at the refreshment breaks.

2. The greatest nuisance (**is** are) the refunds we have to make.

3. Each of the supervisors (**needs** need) a planning calendar.

4. The committee (**has** have) agreed to submit the report next week.

5. Neither the president nor the membership (**was** were) in favor of meeting weekly.

6. Either May or June (**is** are) a good time for the regional conference.

7. This study, as well as many earlier studies, (**shows** show) that turnover is declining steadily.

8. A system of lines (**extends** extend) horizontally to form a grid.

9. The panel, consisting of outstanding representatives from private industry and government, (**has agreed** have agreed) to accept questions on the report.

10. Everybody in the meeting (**was** were) becoming restless as the discussion continued.

✍ EXERCISE SIX—AGREEMENT AND PRONOUNS

Your proofread memo should look like this.

To: All Department Supervisors
From: Erika Chandler, CEO

The management team of Sulsen Designs **has** decided to implement a new system throughout the organization: Cross-Functional Work Teams. This innovative approach to cooperative management will be explained and presented in detail at an upcoming meeting for supervisors.

Team is a collective noun and needs a singular verb.

Supervisors are expected to attend the meeting and make a presentation to their departments. Cross-functional work teams are necessary because commercial clients are requiring more personalized service, and residential clients **demand** more diversity.

Non-sexist language

Subject/verb agreement

A consulting team has been working with senior management and **me** to facilitate the transition to this exciting program. If you have any questions before the meeting, please address them to Scooter Mijer, Director of Human Resources, or **me**. We will speak to **whoever** has specific, logistical concerns.

Pronoun: me is the object of the preposition with.

Pronoun: me is the object of the preposition to.

Who/whom: substitute "He has concerns."

✍ EXERCISE SEVEN—PUNCTUATION ERRORS

The following are the punctuation marks you should have added.

Are you ready to put your punctuation knowledge to the test? Read through this document once before making any proofreaders' marks. Then go back and put in any necessary punctuation marks. As you can already tell, there are no punctuation marks at all; you get to test your proofreading for punctuation errors. Have fun!

Punctuation marks have often been compared to road signs. They direct the reader through the document. Imagine if you were driving through your city's streets, and there were no traffic signs; chaos would result! It's important to use the appropriate signs, and then your reader will quickly and efficiently be able to read and comprehend your document. Don't you find it rather difficult reading this exercise with no punctuation marks?

The punctuation marks you'll use most frequently are as follows: period, comma, semicolon, parentheses, question mark, apostrophe, and quotation marks. Did I leave any out? Look over your document one more time, and make sure you've caught all the errors.

✍ EXERCISE EIGHT—USAGE ERRORS

Did you circle the appropriate word?

1. We are (anxious, **eager**) to participate in the sales training program.

2. The service representative (**assured**, ensured, insured) the customer that the shipment would arrive on schedule.

3. There is a conflict (among, **between**) operations and marketing.

4. The reorganization will (**affect**, effect) the home office as well as the regional offices.

5. When you are finished with the reports, please (**lay**, lie) them on my desk.

6. You may be able to provide (consul, council, **counsel**) to Marie since you have attended the officers' meetings in the past.

7. Do you (**imply**, infer) by your complaints that you don't want to use the new computer software program?

8. The Sales Department has set its goals (farther, **further**) than the Marketing Department.

9. The computer (**continually**, continuously) breaks down.

10. I suggest that you (**accept**, except) the job offer from the West Coast.

11. (Its, **It's**) going to take four weeks for the new equipment to arrive.

12. The committee decided it will need more (**capital**, capitol) to finance the new product line.

13. To receive a higher rating on your next performance evaluation, you will need to make (**fewer**, less) mistakes in your work.

14. I no sooner began my briefing (**than**, then) Fred interrupted me.

15. Follow this (**advice**, advise): get to work on time.

16. We are (**all ready**, already) to begin work on the Fullerton project.

17. His humor is the perfect (**complement**, compliment) to my seriousness.

EXERCISE EIGHT (continued)

18. Our nonprofit organization just received a large endowment from its (principal, principle) benefactor.

19. The next time you order (stationary, stationery) for our office, use the telephone by the (stationary, stationery) terminal.

20. If you disagree with the proposal, be sure to (cite, site, sight) your reasons.

21. Ask the accountants to (set, sit) their materials in the next office.

22. As a (disinterested, uninterested) member, she can give an objective decision.

23. Managers must use (their, there, they're) judgment when disciplining employees.

24. Remember that you (emigrate, immigrate) from a country and (emigrate, immigrate) into a country.

25. Service, not price, is the main (criteria, criterion) we use when we make our purchasing decisions.

✍ EXERCISE NINE—CAPITALIZATION

In the following letter, did you capitalize the appropriate words?

Senator Grant Jones
State Capitol
6421 Sacramento Street, **N.W.**
Sacramento, California 62111

Dear Senator Jones:

This letter is to inform you of the opposition of the California Retailers Association to Senate Bill 1246.

As you are aware, we represent the majority of all retail businesses in California. Some of our more prominent members are Samson's, Short Drug Stores, Capital Camera, Derby Corporation, and all divisions of Acme Department Stores.

Our members are concerned with the provision of the bill that would exempt out-of-state mail order firms from a state sales tax. This matter was discussed at our spring legislative conference held in San Diego at the Hilton Hotel. The membership of the association voted unanimously to oppose Senate Bill 1246 because of this provision.

For example, we are concerned that companies such as Austin Express and Sparrow's Computer Corporation are able to mail their products into California and not incur any state sales tax. Also, this bill does not even address the issue of local sales taxes such as those in West Los Angeles County.

Senator, we appreciate your assistance in this matter and look forward to meeting with you.

Sincerely

Chuck Billkiller
Executive Vice President
California Retailers Association

✍ EXERCISE TEN—NUMBERS

Did you catch all the errors in number usage?

To: Tony R. Sifuentes
From: Carol E. Fisher
Subject: Formal Disciplinary Hearings Scheduled for July **10–13**

The agency's calendar for July includes the dates of July **10**, **11**, **12**, and **13** for formal disciplinary hearings. Because of the length of time of hearings each day (**8** a.m.–**6** p.m.), we are having problems securing hotel space for the hearings. Most of the hotels we have contacted will only commit the meeting space from **9** a.m.–**5** p.m.

Yesterday my administrative assistant contacted the Joe C. Thompson Conference Center, 4455 **Third** Street in Austin to determine whether it had suitable space available for July **10–13**. She indicated that they had a meeting room **150** feet by **50** feet that is available. There is also no restriction on time limit for use of the room if we conclude the hearings by **7** p.m. each day.

The **one** problem I see is that **80** students from th University of Houston College of Pharmacy may want to attend two days of the hearings. Since this room can accommodate only **thirty**-odd members of the class, I suggest we videotape the hearings. The other **50** can view the selected hearing at a later date.

Since the agency does not own the equipment to videotape the proceedings, I would suggest that we contract for this service. **Four** vendors are available, but **two** of the **four** bids look the most attractive. Audio-Visual Productions has quoted $350.**00** for **one 8**-hour hearing, and Sound Systems has quoted $349.50. Each requires **one-fourth** of the total amount as a deposit.

Since time is running short, please contact me by Friday, the 15th of May, so that I can brief you on the specific cases that will be heard in July. If you need to discuss this matter with me on May **6** or **7**, I will be in Washington, D.C. at the Fairmont Hotel, **Two** Lexington Avenue, 202/961-3500.

PROOFREADER'S POST TEST

ONLY ACTION IS ACTION—
PUTTING YOUR SKILLS TO PRACTICE!

Dear Proofreader:

Congratulations! **Y**ou've completed the ***Powerful Proofreading Skills*** book. **A**re you ready to put your new or refreshed skills to the test**?** Here we go.

As you may already **kn**ow, communication skills are critical for success in the business world. **Y**our written and verbal communication skills are a representation of *you* on a daily basis. A promotion or salary increase may be tied to your ability to be accurate and efficient at your workplace.

Let's look back at what you've learned. **Y**our workbook covered the following topics: proofreading tips and strategies, proofreaders' marks, grammar, punctuation, capitalization, numbers vs. words, spelling, and usage. Wow! That's **a l**ot of material to cover in just one d**ay**. Perhaps some **in**formation was new to you; perhaps some was simp**ly** a refresher of material you learned years ago.

Your co-workers and supervisor **are** going to be **eager** to see you produce error-free documents. **B**est of success to you in your business correspondence.

RECOMMENDED READING

Anderson, Laura Killen. *Handbook for Proofreading.* Lincolnwood, Ill.: NTC Business Books, 1990.

Baugh, L. Sue. *Essentials of English Grammar.* Lincolnwood, Ill.: Passport Books, 1990.

Boston, Bruce O. *Stet! Tricks of the Trade for Writers and Editors.* Alexandria, Va.: Editorial Experts, Inc., 1986.

Dewar, Thadys Johnson and H. Francis Daniels. *Programmed Proofreading.* Cincinnati, Ohio: Southwestern Publishing Co., 1987.

Freeman, Morton S. *The Wordwatcher's Guide to Good Writing and Grammar.* Cincinnati, Ohio: Writer's Digest Books, 1990.

Hooper, Vincent F., Cedric Gale, Ronald C. Foote, and Benjamin W. Griffith. *Essentials of English.* Hauppauge, N.Y.: Barrons' Educational Series, 1990.

Ivers, Mitchell. *The Random House Guide to Good Writing.* New York: Random House, 1991.

Judd, Karen. *Copyediting: A Practical Guide.* Menlo Park, Calif.: Crisp Publications, 1988.

Osborn, Patricia. *How Grammar Works.* New York: John Wiley & Sons, 1989.

Sabin, William A. *The Gregg Reference Manual.* Westerville, Ohio: Macmillan/McGraw-Hill, 1992.

Shertzer, Margaret D. *The Elements of Grammar.* New York: Macmillan Publishing Co., 1986.

Smith, Peggy. *Simplified Proofreading.* Alexandria, Va.: Editorial Experts, 1987.

————. *Mark My Words.* Alexandria, Va.: Editorial Experts, 1989.

Strunk, William, and E. B. White. *The Elements of Style.* New York: Macmillan Publishing Co., 1979.

University of Chicago Press. *The Chicago Manual of Style.* Chicago, Ill.: University of Chicago Press, 1982.

Venolia, Jan. *Write Right!* Woodland Hills, Calif.: Periwinkle Press, 1985.

————. *Rewrite Right!* Berkeley, Calif.: Ten Speed Press, 1987.

U.S. Government Printing Office. *A Manual of Style.* New York: Gramercy Publishing Co., 1986.

NOTES

NOTES

NOTES

NOTES

NOW AVAILABLE FROM CRISP PUBLICATIONS

Books•Videos•CD-ROMs•Computer-Based Training Products

Subject Areas Include:

Management
Human Resources
Communication Skills
Personal Development
Marketing/Sales
Organizational Development
Customer Service/Quality
Computer Skills
Small Business and Entrepreneurship
Adult Literacy and Learning
Life Planning and Retirement

7/98

CRISP WORLDWIDE DISTRIBUTION

English language books are distributed worldwide. Major international distributors include:

ASIA/PACIFIC

Australia/New Zealand: In Learning, PO Box 1051, Springwood QLD, Brisbane, Australia 4127   Tel: 61-7-3-841-2286, Facsimile: 61-7-3-841-1580
ATTN: Messrs. Gordon

Philippines: Management Review Publishing, Inc., 301 Tito Jovey Center, Buencamino Str., Alabang, Muntinlupa, Metro Manila, Philippines   Tel: 632-842-3092,
E-mail: robert@easy.net.ph
ATTN: Mr. Trevor Roberts

Japan: Phoenix Associates Co., LTD., Mizuho Bldng, 3-F, 2-12-2, Kami Osaki, Shinagawa-Ku, Tokyo 141   Tel: 81-33-443-7231, Facsimile: 81-33-443-7640
ATTN: Mr. Peter Owans

CANADA

Reid Publishing, Ltd., Box 69559, 60 Briarwood Avenue, Port Credit, Ontario, Canada L5G 3N6   Tel: (905) 842-4428, Facsimile: (905) 842-9327
ATTN: Mr. Steve Connolly / Mr. Jerry McNabb

Trade Book Stores: Raincoast Books, 8680 Cambie Street, Vancouver, B.C., V6P 6M9
Tel: (604) 323-7100, Facsimile: (604) 323-2600
ATTN: Order Desk

EUROPEAN UNION

England: Flex Training, Ltd., 9-15 Hitchin Street, Baldock, Hertfordshire, SG7 6A, England   Tel: 44-1-46-289-6000, Facsimile: 44-1-46-289-2417
ATTN: M. David Willetts

INDIA

Multi-Media HRD, Pvt., Ltd., National House, Tulloch Road, Appolo Bunder, Bombay, India 400-039   Tel: 91-22-204-2281, Facsimile: 91-22-283-6478
ATTN: Messrs. Aggarwal

MEXICO

Grupo Editorial Iberoamerica, Nebraska 199, Col. Napoles, 03810 Mexico, D.F.
Tel: 525-523-0994, Facsimile: 525-543-1173
ATTN: Señor Nicholas Grepe

SOUTH AFRICA

Alternative Books, PO Box 1345, Ferndale 2160, South Africa
Tel: 27-11-792-7730, Facsimile: 27-11-792-7787
ATTN: Mr. Vernon de Haas